Hold to Your Dream

Hold to Your Dream

HELEN LOWRIE MARSHALL

Doubleday & Company, Inc. Garden City, New York

To Vern
Who has given me so much

And with special thanks to
Dr. Frank A. Court
and
The Rev. George L. Davis

"Dream manfully and nobly,
and thy dreams shall be prophets."
—*Sir Edw. Bulwer-Lytton*

ISBN: 0-385-08260-6

Library of Congress Catalog Card Number 65–29051
Copyright © 1965 by Helen Lowrie Marshall
All Rights Reserved
Printed in the United States of America

9   8   7

Contents

Hold to Your Dream

A dream is a high and lovely thing,
A heart-flown kite on the winds of Spring.
Buoyant and bright, it hovers there
Against the blue—almost a prayer,
Calling the spirit to broaden its scope
Of faith in the future, and courage, and hope;
Adding dimensions of height and girth
To even the simplest joys of earth.

If you have a dream, oh, how lucky you are!
Play out the string and let it sail far,
But follow it—ever so close—with your eyes,
For dreams have been known to be lost in the skies.
Never lose sight of it—hold fast the string—
A dream is a precious and wonderful thing!

Success Is a Journey

Success is a journey—not an end,
   Never a destination.
Success is a good day's work well done,
   Success is preparation,
A fearless facing up to life
   With purpose all the way.
Success is not a distant thing,
   Success is everyday.

The goal—the far horizon—
   Is but the guiding light
That points the way our lives must go
   If we would reach the height;
But never does success await
   That last triumphant climb—
Success is step on upward step—
   Our journey into time.

And if we never quite attain
   That goal—that distant crest—
We have not failed if we've kept faith
   And lived each day our best.

The Splendid Urge

There is a splendid urge all dreamers know,
A splendid, driving urge to live—to grow!
To fling the dream ahead and follow through—
A splendid, thrilling urge to be—to do!

And never did this world have greater need
Of men to dream great dreams, and hearts to heed
That urge to scale the heights not scaled before,
That splendid urge that bids the spirit soar.

If you've a dream—hold fast, nor doubt its scope;
One dream held high can rouse a whole world's hope.
One life, dream-powered, with a will to climb,
Can lift the faith of men to heights sublime.

A splendid urge—would that we all might know
That urge to do—to be—to live—to grow!

If I Should Stumble

If I should stumble—as I have and will,
Oh, let me stumble going up the hill;
Let the stumbling be because my eyes
Are fixed upon some star high in the skies.

If I should fall—and I will have my share,
Let me fall going up the stair;
And let me not blame others for the pain,
But quietly arise and try again.

If I should stumble, let it be I seek
A precious foothold toward a mountain peak;
Or that I feel the challenge of the pace
Set by fleeter runners in life's race.

If I should stumble on my little mile,
Help me to make that stumbling worthwhile,
To recognize the blocks that fouled my way
And thus climb better on the coming day.

Isn't Life Glorious

Isn't life glorious! Isn't it grand!
Here—take it—hold it tight in your hand;
Squeeze every drop of it into your soul,
Drink of the joy of it, sun-sweet and whole!
Laugh with the love of it, burst into song!
Scatter its richness as you stride along!
Isn't life splendid—and isn't it great
We can always start living—it's never too late!

The Privilege of Living

Thank God for the privilege of living,
The privilege of breathing the air,
The privilege of being alive in the midst
Of such beauty everywhere!
Thank the good Lord for His mercy
In giving me eyes to see,
A mind to learn, and a voice to speak
And a faith in Eternity.
Thank God for the privilege of living—
For sharing His earth and His sky—
That a gift so rare as the gift of life
Is given to such as I.

A Certain Aura

I love to see him walk. He never saunters,
For there is always purpose in his stride,
A buoyant joy in living there—a firmness,
A faith in life that gives him strength and pride.

He wears a cloak of confidence around him
As dashing as a cape on knight of old,
And yet his gentle smile belies his vigor—
It is his faith alone that makes him bold.

I love to watch him walk, for there is something
About his stride—his smile—his genial nod
That lends a certain aura to his passing—
You know you've seen a man who walks with God.

A *Faith to Live By*

Give me the faith of adventure, Lord,
  The courage to try the new,
The will to press on in spite of the dark,
  Knowing I walk with You.

Give me the faith of desire and hope,
  The inward urge to achieve.
All things are possible with You.
  O Lord, let me believe!

Give me the faith of awareness
  Of beauty everywhere,
Eyes to see, and ears to hear—
  An open heart to care.

Give me a faith to *live* by,
  Joyous and unafraid,
A glorious faith to match the dawn
  Of this day You have made!

Reach High!

Reach high! The finest things of life
Are on the topmost shelves.
We have to stand on tiptoe—
Stretch our small, self-centered selves;
We have to look above our heads
To where the heart can see,
If we would reach that finer life
We'd like our life to be.

We have to mount our old mistakes
And try and try again
If we would even touch
Life's highest moments now and then—
If we would even brush with lightest
Fingertips the best
That life on earth can offer—
If we would reach the crest.

Reach high! The best is always kept
Upon life's topmost shelves,
But not beyond our reach if we
Will reach beyond ourselves.

The Living Church

This, then, is the church—not brick nor stone,
Nor leaded pane, nor heaven-pointed spire.
If we would see the real church we must look
Fathoms deeper, infinitely higher,
Beyond the narrow borders of our sight,
For boundless and eternal is its scope—
Wide as the very love of God is wide,
As deep as faith, unquenchable as hope.

Within the hearts and lives of those who've known
Its healing touch, its power to remold,
It walks the streets of life, a living thing,
To challenge and inspire young and old.
Through you and me, and Christians everywhere,
The living church moves on, an endless chain—
The touch of life on life—a heritage
Of riches deepening with every strain.

No stationary monument is this,
For, be it humble room or work of art,
The church is only real as it becomes
God's gift of love passed on from heart to heart.

Here and there, and now and then
God plants a giant among men
That such as you and I may see
The height of true nobility;
A giant spurring lesser men
To polish up their dreams again;
A giant calling smaller souls
To dredge up long-forgotten goals;
A giant men may look upon,
As men have looked upon the dawn—
The weak, the bitter, the oppressed,
With new hope rising in their breast;
A measure of what man can be
Who prizes human dignity.

(From Kennedy "Commemorative Anthology")

The Lone Star-Maker

He was a lone star-maker,
Holding his small light
High aloft in the darkness
Of a world lost in the night.

Trying there to penetrate
The fog that blurred men's eyes—
A candle held courageously
Against the starless skies.

His was a lonesome business,
Unheralded—unpraised—
A single candle-light of truth
In blackest darkness raised.

He was a lone star-maker,
But that one star held high,
Broke through the clouded hearts of men
And lit the whole dark sky.

Pot of Gold

We all know the old, old story
  Of the pot of gold to be found
Where the glorious arch of the rainbow
  Dips and touches the ground.

We all know it's only a story,
  A beautiful fantasy,
But perhaps it holds a word to the wise
  If we really look to see.

For sure it is that a pot of gold
  Is waiting for him whose eyes
Are lifted up to the promise of hope
  Of a rainbow in the skies.

A treasure of golden hours of peace—
  True measure of success,
For the heart with faith in the beauty of life—
  The secret of happiness.

And he who follows the rainbow trail
  And accepts its challenging quest,
Will find there is really a pot of gold
  If he gives to the world his best.

Love-Wide and Heaven-High

My world was little and cozy-tight,
Snug and smug in its dim half-light;
And, though it was too small inside
For me to stretch my arms out wide
Or let me stand up straight and tall,
This annoyed me not at all.
I crouched in my small world each day,
Content to doze the hours away—
Till a stray sunbeam, quite lost, I'm sure,
Found its way through a crack in my door.
A wandering thought it might have been,
But it shone with a brightness I'd never seen,
And it lighted my world's dimlit way
And it tempted me forth to a sunbright day.
I opened the door and stepped outside
Into a new world, high and wide!
With outstretched arms to embrace it all,
I felt my soul stand straight and tall!
And I knew that I could never go back
To that little world with its pitiful lack
Of all that made life glow and shine,
Now that this wider world was mine.
So I closed the door and I turned the key
On that little world and that little me,
And I raised my face to the open sky
In a world love-wide and Heaven-high!

High, Wide and Handsome

High and wide and handsome—
  That's how life should be;
Wide and high as a prairie sky,
  Open and clean and free.

Handsomely giving of ourselves
  And that which bears our brand,
Sharing the best of what we possess
  With a big and generous hand.

No more fences of fear and hate
  Dividing the human race;
Giving our minds the run of the range
  In God's great open space.

High and wide and handsome,
  Honest and clean and free,
A young-as-spring, adventuresome thing—
  Life should, and life can, be!

Dare to Be Different

Dare to be different; life is so full
Of people who follow the same push-and-pull,
Poor, plodding people who, other than name,
Try to pretend they're exactly the same.

God made men different; there never will be
A replica soul made of you or of me.
The charm—the glory of all creation
Rests on this very deviation.

Your charm—your own glory, too,
Lies in being uniquely you—
Lies in being true to your best,
That part of you different from all of the rest.

Sometimes a Star

May the rains of life that fall upon
    Your spirits now and then,
Leave behind them pools of light
    To make life bright again,
Clean and shining pools of light
    Reflecting Heaven's blue,
And possibly sometimes a star
    To light the way for you.

21

Co-Creators

I'm glad God leaves a part
Of His creation up to me;
I'm glad He puts a challenge here
And gives me eyes to see
The part that I must play—
The work my hands alone must do
To bring about this portion
Of creation, fresh and new.

I'm glad that He sees fit to use
My small and humble gifts
To channel through to others
A bit of that which lifts;
I'm glad He's made of me
An instrument that I might give
A helping hand that others
More abundantly might live.

I'm glad He merely plants the seed
Then leaves it up to me
To cultivate the finished deed
Of better things to be.
I'm glad, so glad, to have a share
In adding to the worth,
The beauty and the glory
Of creation here on earth.

A Heaven Every Day

What wondrous miracles abound
  In ordinary things,
And yet how casually we see
  And hear a world that sings.
A rosebud bursts its prison pod
  And fragrance fills the air—
The tender grasses break the sod
  And green is everywhere.

A daisy lifts its dazzling smile
  To blue skies high above—
A maiden plucks the petals off
  And dreams of her true love.
A baby takes a faltering step—
  A brave soul smiles through pain.
The summer dies—the white snow flies—
  And spring is •born again.

A universe of miracles,
  So very commonplace
We take them all for granted
  And accept with careless grace.
With wistful eyes we visualize
  A Heaven far away,
The while we stumble blindly through
  A heaven every day.

Are You Fishing for Dreams?

Are you fishing for dreams? Then bait your hook
  With a bit of reality,
Then swing out wide and cast your line
  Far out into Life's sea.

Let every dream have a fighting chance,
  Give it plenty of slack,
But settle for only the biggest and best—
  Throw the little ones back.

Are you fishing for dreams? Then I wish you luck,
  It's a good dream-fishing day.
May you catch a beauty—but oh, take care,
  Lest the big one get away.

The Song of Life

The music of life is played by ear,
Each heart improvising its own,
Setting the tempo and choosing the key
In major or minor tone.

No printed score is provided,
And no two tunes the same;
And if our song is discordant,
We've only ourselves to blame.

For the keyboard of life holds beauty—
There's harmony waiting there
For the heart that attunes its song of life
To peace, goodwill and prayer.

A Dream Is Forever

A dream is forever—spurn it if you will—
Somewhere in your heart there's a part of it still;
Somewhere there's an echo—a smile or a sigh,
Recalling that long-ago dream that passed by.

A dream is forever—it can't be erased;
And richer the life that a dream has embraced,
Warmer the heart that has felt the bright beam
Of life-giving hope shining forth in a dream.

What a Difference

What a difference a dream can make—
It can alter the whole way life may take,
It can give us the power and courage to do
Whatever is needed to see our way through.
It can color our thinking and brighten our days.
It can change our lives in a thousand ways.
A dream can lend credence and beauty and glory
To every chapter of anyone's story.
A dream is worth trying, if just for the sake
Of seeing the difference a great dream can make.

Back From the Road

Let me go back from the traveled road
Away from the crowds pushing by,
To a quiet hill where the woods are still,
Serene 'neath a clean, blue sky.

I would go back, far back from the road,
Away from the haunts of men,
I would find peace of mind where the hidden
    trails wind,
And strength to return again.

A Faith That Smiles

Give us a faith in the worth of ourselves,
And faith in our fellowman;
Give us a faith that right will prevail
In the Infinite over-all plan;
Give us a faith in the future—
A farmer's faith in the sod,
A faith in Eternal justice,
A faith in the love of God;
Give us a faith for the journey of life,
A strength for the winding miles,
A faith to sustain—but above all, Lord,
Give us a faith that smiles!

Reflections

Folks are about as nice, I find,
As I let them be, in my own mind.
Let me be in an ugly mood
And I find them all impossibly rude!
But let me wake feeling warm and mellow
And everyone is a charming fellow!
Grim or gracious, that's the kind
Of grim or gracious folks I find,
For everyone I meet, you see,
Reflects a little bit of me.

Never Afraid

He, who has once caught sight of a star
Is never afraid of the dark,
For always, through Life's blackest night
He carries with him the spark,
The tiny glow that will guide him
Unerringly toward his goal.
He who has once caught sight of a star
Is master of his soul.

For a dream—a noble endeavor—
Is God's own light that shines
Deep in the heart of the trusting soul
Whose faith that dream enshrines;
And neither storm nor black of night
Can dim that God-lit spark—
He who has once caught sight of a star
Is never afraid of the dark.

Whatever Your Gift

What is that you hold in your hand?
Nothing, you say? Look again.
Every hand holds some special gift—
A hammer, a broom, a pen,
A hoe, a scalpel, an artist's brush,
A needle, a microscope,
A violin's bow, a way with words
In the giving of faith and hope.
What is that you hold in your hand?
Whatever your gift may be,
It can open your door to abundant life—
You hold in your hand the key.

One Thing More

We may know love, respect, compassion, care,
But, lacking one more thing, our life is bare.
Unless we feel we're needed here on earth,
All else will be of very little worth.
Unless we have an opportunity
To live the Golden Rule, our life will be
An empty thing, unhappy at the core—
The human soul demands this one thing more.
We may know love, respect, compassion, care,
But let us have another's cross to share,
A brother's burden we can help to pull—
Then, only, will our life be meaningful.

Always There

Bless those folks who are "always there,"
  Steadfast, loyal and true,
Standing by and happy to share
  Your joys and your cares with you.

Those who stand on the side and cheer
  The runners in life's race,
Whose faith supplies the needed boost
  To keep that winning pace.

Bless those backstage people,
  Whose art no plaudits rouse,
But who provide the background
  For those who take the bows.

Bless them all—those quiet ones,
  Steady and staunch and square,
The little matches that light the stars—
  The folks who are "always there."

A Lovely Day

Actually, I couldn't say
What made this such a lovely day.
The air was chill, the clouds hung low,
Yet it was lovely—that I know.
Perhaps it was because someone
Smiled my way and brought the sun;
Maybe it was only that
A friend stopped for a little chat;
Or that a neighbor passing by
Called a warm and friendly "Hi!"
Possibly its special glow
Came from helping one I know—
Not much really—just a hand
To let him know I understand.
Nothing happened, actually,
To set this day apart for me.
Things went along the usual way—
But oh, it's been a lovely day!

No Farther Away Than Today

No farther away
Than Here and Today
Is the loveliest place I know—
A small secret spot
In a walled garden plot
Where all the nice memories grow.

It's bordered with kindness
And sprinkled with smiles
And shaded by friendly trees—
This small quiet place
In that walled garden space
With its bright little memories.

And I think about this—
How, if I were to miss
One day with my rake and my hoe
In planting the seeds
Of a few kindly deeds,
It would mean fewer memories to grow.

So I try every hour
To plant a new flower,
And strike down a weed in the way
Where the nice memories grow
In that spot that I know
No farther than Here and Today.

Sunday in June

There's a very special difference
In a Sunday morn in June—
A sort of singing stillness,
As though all life's in tune,
As though all nature's joining
In a reverent hymn of praise
To Him whose loving-kindness
Has provided such rare days.
There's a gentleness that lingers
On the tranquil Sabbath air,
A calm, a peace that hovers
Over all things everywhere—
A very special difference—
A whole new world reborn
In the hushed and holy quiet
Of a June-time Sunday morn.

Prelude

The harmony of Heaven fills the air,
As softly now the organ lifts its prayer.

A Poet Thinks

I cannot help but wonder why
God chose a person such as I
To point the ways of right and wrong,
Equipped with nothing but a song.

So strange that this small gift of mine
Seems part of His great plan divine;
Strange He should use my tongue and pen
To reach the hearts and souls of men.

Why give me words to weave His spell—
And wit to weave them passing well—
When my own heart is fearful still,
Rebellious, often, to His will?

I can but pray that as I go
With words to help these others grow,
I, too, may grow in faith to be
More worthy of His faith in me.

Out of Their Love

Father in Heaven, please forgive
This halo that I wear.
So blinded by their love for me
Are they who put it there;
So blind with love they cannot see
How awkwardly it fits,
And with what incongruity
Upon my head it sits.
They cannot see how very apt it is
To slip and fall,
How carefully I have to walk
To keep it there at all.
Somehow I think You understand—
Although I know, inside,
How wrong it is, I wear it still
With dignity and pride.
Those trusting hearts who fashioned it
Out of their love for me
Must never know how ill it fits
And how precariously.

A Minute to Spend

So you have only a minute to spend?
Well, here's what a minute will buy—
A word to let someone know that you care,
A smile to a passerby,
A bit of communion with God and His world,
A "thank you" that's maybe long due,
A deep look inward to change your sights
And broaden your point of view.
If you have all of a minute to spend,
How very lucky you are!
For a minute will buy a whole heart's prayer,
And pay your way clean to a star!

My Day

This be my day—
Some honest work,
A bit of play—
To laugh and love,
And live and pray
With God beside me
All the way—
This be my day.

My Cameos of Memory

These are my treasures kept apart,
Cradled in velvet in my heart,
Graven profiles, picture-clear,
Perfect moments, priceless-dear,
Etched in ageless time to be
    My cameos of memory.

The hours I have spent with you,
The tender times, the fun times, too,
The summer roses and the rain,
The laughter and the precious pain
Of loving you—your loving me—
    My cameos of memory.

These are my wealth, my warmth, my light,
I keep them dream-close all the night.
With finger-tips of heart and mind
I trace each profile there defined—
These treasures none can take from me—
    My cameos of memory.

Strange—but the more I know of you,
The better I like myself.
You always seem to take the book
Of Me down off the shelf,
And turn the pages of my mind
Until you make me see
The finer, bigger, happier sort
Of person I might be.
I grow an inch or two in height
Each time you look my way.
You exhilarate my ego—
I feel happy—I feel gay.
And quite the nicest part of all—
And this is very true—
The more I like myself—the more
I love the world and you.

Enduring Grateful

There's an old, old phrase
That is warm and true,
And expresses a thought sincere—
"Enduring grateful"—and that I am
To you for your words of cheer;
"Enduring grateful" for all the times
You've found to lend a hand;
"Enduring grateful" for the way
You always understand.
A simple and old-fashioned phrase,
But in its own quaint way
It says exactly how I feel
And what I'd like to say.

A Halo on the Head

Man must have his earth-god to look up to,
Must build an image of his own ideal,
And, though the virtues crowned are most unworthy,
In his adoring eyes they're true and real.
And, strangely, though of purest fancy fashioned,
A halo on the head placed there by love,
Imparts a nobleness to him who wears it,
A certain kinship with the saints above.

Only a Moment

It was only a moment—a glimpse—a gleam,
A fleet-winged fancy, a wisp of a dream,
But it etched its mark forever to be
A part of this God-patterned clay called me.

Only a moment, clutched at and gone,
Only a memory lingering on,
But swiftly and surely it traced its line
On this God-given mind and heart of mine.

Only a moment—one bit of light
Flickering dim in the midst of the night,
But in that moment it left its scroll
On this God-fashioned thing I call my soul.

Gentle Valor

There is a valiant gentleness about her;
You know that trouble has not passed her by,
But life will never vanquish her completely,
For there is still a twinkle in her eye.

When Winter Comes

When winter comes, I shall remember
  This glorious day in May.
In the chill of life's coldest December,
  I shall be warmed that way.

I shall be warmed by the sunshine
  Of a world attuned to Spring;
I shall see apple trees in bloom,
  I shall hear robins sing.

No matter how the winds buffet,
  No matter how deep the snow,
Life's beauty outweighs its bitter—
  Remembering—I shall know.

Tomorrow's Time Enough

Tomorrow's time enough for growing old.
First, we must spend Today's full cup of gold.
These freshly minted minutes, hundreds strong—
Why buy a sigh when they will buy a song?
Thousands of shining seconds—each will buy
A breath of clean, fresh air, a patch of sky,
A warming clasp of hand, a flashing smile—
What treasures for one second's little while!
Such wealth we have to spend—a whole Today!
Tomorrow is a long, long time away.

You Never Know

You never know when someone
May catch a dream from you.
You never know when a little word
Or something you may do
May open up the windows
Of a mind that seeks the light—
The way you live may not matter at all,
But you never know—it might.

And just in case it could be
That another's life, through you,
Might possibly change for the better
With a broader and brighter view,
It seems it might be worth a try
At pointing the way to the right—
Of course, it may not matter at all,
But then again—it might.

These We Have Known

These we have known together—
 Hundreds of happy hours,
Beautiful, bright blue weather,
 Rainbows following showers.

Comfortable silence, and laughter,
 So many shared memories—
No matter what follows after,
 Nothing can take away these.

Small private jokes and the stories
 Amusing to us alone;
Life's little triumphs and glories,
 Marking each happy milestone.

Dreams that we shared in the making,
 And watching a few come true;
Failures the easier taking
 Because we were always two.

Love in its full completeness,
 Life its abundant best—
Nothing can alter the sweetness—
 We have been truly blest.

On a Lonely Hill

On a lonely hill I stood alone
   Against a mourning sky,
In a grief-filled world I'd never known
   With none to hear my cry.

Racked with pain, heart-broken, ill,
   I stood alone with my loss,
Till it seemed I saw another hill
   And a Man on a cruel cross.

He, too, had stood on a lonely hill
   In pain that would not cease,
And I heard Him say, "My child, be still,
   I give to you My peace."

"Not as the world gives, do I give—
   The world may not understand—
But I say unto you that you can live
   With this grief—if you take My hand."

I came down out of the lonely hill,
   And my sorrow found release—
My hand in His, my will His Will,
   And in my heart His peace.

Putting Out the Lamp

Death is not extinguishing the light—
Blank darkness when the spark of life is gone;
It, rather, is an ending of the night,
A putting out the lamp at break of dawn.

Just softly putting out the little lamp
That burns within this life to light our way,
A lamp no longer needed when the dawn
Has come to usher in that brighter day.

No, death is not extinguishing the light—
No settling down of dark when life is gone;
Death is only putting out the lamp—
A lifting of the shade to greet the dawn.

Only Me

My neighbor does not see the Christ,
    His cross, His Calvary.
My neighbor stands across the way
    And watches only me.

My neighbor does not hear His word,
    But oh, how closely he
Takes heed of how I bear my cross
    And meet my Calvary.

45

God Is a Gracious Landlord

God is a gracious landlord;
   His generosity
Is equalled only by His boundless
   Love for you and me.

Were we to list His many gifts
   Laid up to our account,
We could not write them fast enough,
   So quickly they would mount.

Then, would we list our gifts to Him
   And those made in His name,
I wonder—could we view those lists
   Without a sense of shame?

God is a gracious landlord,
   His giving knows no dearth—
How great our privilege to be
   His stewards here on earth.

An Ordinary Day

Today was just an ordinary day—
I went about my tasks the usual way;
The path was one that I had often trod,
But oh, the difference—
  Now I walk with God.

Today was just an ordinary day
And nothing special happened on the way,
But oh, the inner joy you didn't see,
Now that I know my Savior
  Walks with me!

Today was just an ordinary day,
The usual work, and then a bit of play,
But oh, the sense of peace at eventide
To know that God and I walk
  Side by side!

God Give Us Growth

God give us growth—a deeper joy in serving,
A fuller understanding of Thy will;
A firm and constant faith that knows no swerving,
The courage our commitments to fulfill.

Give us to grow in spiritual insight,
Make keener our awareness of the power
Of prayer to turn the darkness into daylight
And give us strength to meet each trying hour.

We would expand the compass of our thinking
To gather in its scope the whole world's need;
To recognize the Christian interlinking
Of every race and color, class and creed.

God give us growth—each day in all our living
That we may feel Thy presence over all,
Thy blessing on each service—every giving.
God give us growth till we be Heaven-tall.

My Church Home

This is my home, my church home,
  The place where I belong,
Where friends and loved ones join with me
  In praise and prayer and song.

This is my home, my church home,
  With doors that open wide,
Where I can come when cares beset
  And know love waits inside.

This is my home, my church home,
  My haven from the storm,
Where friendly hands reach out to me,
  Gracious and true and warm.

This is my home, my church home—
  Oh, would that I could share
Its strength and love and peace and joy
  With all folk everywhere.

My Wish for You

One wish I hold in my heart for you—
Not that all of your dreams come true,
(Though surely I hope for more than a few),
Not that you never may know a care,
(But oh, never more than your heart can bear),
Not that your life may hold happiness only,
Or that you may never be burdened or lonely,
For life without sorrow—a life without giving—
Is but half a life that is truly worth living.
No, my wish for you encompasses more—
May there always be something for you to wish for.

The Most Important Words

The most important words in the world
Are the words that we say to ourself.
Far more important than all of the words
In the loftiest books on our shelf
Are the quiet sayings the still, small voice
Deep down in our inmost soul
Speaks to our heart when we're all alone;
For, no matter what the role
We may choose to play in life's masquerade,
Our gains are but meaningless pelf,
If the glory and richness of life are not ours
In the life that we live with ourself.

Gather Ye Recipes

Gather ye recipes while ye may—
Carefully, carefully tuck them away;
Store them in boxes and paste them in books—
Glamorous dishes of venturesome cooks!

Clip them out, snip them out, fill up the files,
Tie them in bundles and stack them in piles.
Handle them tenderly, treat them with care,
For, if you're like me, they'll lie buried there

For ever and ever (or till you clean house),
While you and your meat-and-potatoes spouse
Will dine on old stand-bys you whip up instead
From the old tried and true that you keep
   in your head.

Helpful Hints

I love those Helpful Hints sent in
  By housewives like myself.
I clip them out and put them
  In a box up on the shelf.
The only trouble is that I
  Can never find the one
That fits the situation
  And corrects the thing I've done.

For instance, one said vinegar (?)
  Takes scorch stains out of clothes—
Or was it salt? Or soda?
  There—you see? That's how it goes.
There's something just a pinch of
  Will keep meringue from weeping.
I can't remember what it was,
  But it seemed well worth keeping.

I'm simply fascinated by
  The clever, little ways
These smart hardworking housewives
  Find to ease their busy days.
I vow to put each one to use
  As, carefully, I read it,
But, somehow, I can never find it
  When I really need it.

The Elf in My Self

I have a little gamin
In one corner of my self,
And I'm embarrassed often
By this impish little elf.

He's apt to pop out suddenly
With something downright rude
Just when I'm trying extra hard
To be especially good.

He's fond of shocking people
Who are proper as can be.
Believe me, it's not funny,
He's a terrible trial to me.

I can't excuse his antics,
He's a rascal and a knave,
And he'll probably stick with me
Till I'm safely in my grave.

But I hope my friends will try
To make allowances, and see
It's the gamin who is naughty,
It isn't really me.

Especially for You

"I made it 'specially for you,"
  He said, and handed me
The dubious daub of color
  He had made for me to see.

A horse? A cat? A fish? A shoe?
  Who quibbles with such art?
No matter what it was I knew
  It came straight from his heart.

I told him it was beautiful—
  I loved his big surprise!
And a million dollars couldn't buy
  That pleased look in his eyes.

"Especially for you"—three words
  Such potent magic hold.
They turn the smallest gift on earth
  To one of purest gold.

Nothing as Clean

Have you known—really known—a boy of ten,
  Or nine, or eight, or seven?
If so, then you know there is nothing quite
  As clean this side of Heaven.

Oh, it's true that he only washes himself
  Under the strictest duress,
And his hair is practically never combed,
  And his clothes are always a mess.

But he looks at you with those honest eyes,
  And he wrinkles that freckled nose,
And he grins that trusting, toothless grin—
  And only his cleanness shows;

Only his wonderful faith in life,
  His glorious zest for living—
The free, open heart of him loving the world,
  Its sins and shortcomings forgiving.

I think the Creator must surely derive
  His deepest and happiest joy
From the clean little soul that shines out
        through the dirt
  On the face of a fun-loving boy.

It's a Girl!

When she arrived—a baby girl,
    She made our joy complete.
A precious little angel—
    All she did was sleep and eat.
Then she began to walk and talk—
    So dear—so daintily,
A perfect little lady—
    Till she was just past three.

But then, oh horrors, what a change
    Befell our cherub child—
Our dainty little girl became
    A tomboy, loud and wild.
She aped her brother, wore his shirts,
    Insisted on blue jeans,
And kept up this mad masquerade
    Right on up through her teens.

The ruffles, frills and petticoats
    Dear to her mother's heart,
She looked upon with deepest scorn,
    This ragman's counterpart.
But then, one day, for no real cause
    That anyone could see,
She cast aside the loathsome jeans
    For femininity!

Her old belligerence restrained,
    Her voice controlled and pleasing,
Demure and shy with lowered eye,
    She took her brother's teasing!
We reveled in her newfound self,
    Though not without alloy—
We'd found our baby girl again
    But she had found a boy!

"Say Hello to Grandma"

Across the miles a tiny "Hi"—
I strain my ears to hear.
"How are you, darling?" "Fine," he says.
I dab away a tear.
Three costly minutes—two small words—
But who can count their worth?
They've proved beyond a doubt that he's
The smartest child on earth!
Three costly minutes—two small words—
A waste of money? Maybe—
But then you're not the Grandma
Of the world's most brilliant baby!

Oh Where, Oh Where!

Oh where, oh where has our Granny gone?
    The Granny we used to know—
With the little lace cap and the soft, cuddly lap,
    Who hummed as she rocked to and fro.

Where is the Granny who lived in the house
    We went to on Thanksgiving Day?
That long-aproned Granny—that wonderful cook?
    That Granny? She went that-a-way.

Now the cap is replaced by a chic little hat
    She picked up her last trip to France,
And the soft, cuddly lap has long given way
    To the calorie battle and pants.

The rocker is empty, for Granny is out
    Campaigning in politics;
The calico apron's a hostess gown now
    For serving meals easy-to-fix.

That lovely grey hair that set her apart
    As one whose years we respected,
Is covered up now by a glorified wig
    So those years aren't even suspected!

That sunbonnet Granny who puttered about
   Her neat, little vegetable rows,
Is out on the green now, putting about
   In shorts and a sun-freckled nose.

There's only one point where the Granny of old
   And the modern Grandmother's the same—
Give her an inch and she'll take a long mile
   Proclaiming her grandchildren's fame.

No matter how worldly, she still thinks her own
   Grandchildren superior creatures.
She'll whip out their pictures on any pretense
   And bore you with all their fine features.

Oh where, oh where has our Granny gone?
   That Granny when we were small?—
Why, really she hasn't gone anywhere—
   She's just modernized—that's all.

So Small a Thing

So small a thing on which to build
   A faith so firmly kept—
A Babe born in a stable crude
   Where restless cattle slept.
One bright star shining down upon
   The place wherein He lay,
To guide the lowly shepherds there
   And show great kings the way.

A simple tale, yet through the years
   Its stark simplicity
Has taken on the richness
   Of a priceless tapestry;
For man has woven into it
   His hopes, his highest dreams,
His love, his fancy, his beliefs,
   His own star's brightest beams.

And from that manger miracle,
   The tapestry has grown—
The richest tale of miracles
   The world has ever known.
So small a thing on which to base
   A whole world's peace and joy—
A bed of straw, a star, a song,
   And one small Baby Boy.

I Was Thinking

I was thinking—when that little Boy
  Was born that Christmas night—
The poor, young thing who mothered Him
  Must have most died with fright
To have to birth her Baby in a place
  So strange and grim.
I hope some women-folk were there
  To help her care for Him.

I hope they brought warm blankets,
  And hushed His baby cries
With tender, crooning woman-words
  And gentle lullabies.
I hope they brought Him little gifts—
  Not frankincense or gold,
But downy little shirts and sox
  To guard Him from the cold.

And when those Kings and shepherds came
  To see her little Lad,
I hope some women-folk stood by
  So it was not too bad.

Those Christmas Mornings

Those Christmas mornings when we were small—
Oh, those are the happiest memories of all!
When you popped awake with the first faint rays
Of the wintry dawn on that day of days;

And the snow and the sky, still starry-eyed,
Made a Christmas card of the world outside—
For always (well, always as I recall)
Christmas Eve brought a fresh snowfall,

And some of it sifted on the sill;
And everything was so hushed and still—
So still that you could plainly hear
Your own heart thumping loud and clear.
"It's come! It's come!" it seemed to say,
"It's Christmas Day! It's Christmas Day!"

The new, sweet, spicy smell of pine
Made chills run up and down your spine,
For that meant there was a Christmas tree—
Although you always knew there would be.

And you recalled how your Dad had said
That everybody should stay in bed
Till the lights were lit and the house was warm,
But one little peek couldn't do any harm.

So you tiptoed out to the head of the stair—
And, sure enough, Santa Claus had been there!
In the misty half-light you could see
The thrilling shape of the Christmas tree,
The packages and the stockings, too—
A wonderful, wonderful dream come true!

All Dad's advice about sleeping late
Forgotten then—for who could wait!
You let out a whoop of purest joy,
And Dad didn't scold, for he once was a boy.

And then—oh, the laughter, the love and the fun—
At long, precious last, Christmas Day had begun!

Candlelight and Starlight

By candlelight and starlight came He then,
To kindle Hope of Peace in hearts of men.
And every Christmas candle on the sill
Reminds the world that Hope is burning still.
We see a promise in its glowing beam
Of one day the fulfillment of that dream.
By candlelight and starlight came He then;
May star and candle light His way again.

Down Paths of Light and Laughter

Now—may the warming love of friends
  Surround you as you go
Down paths of light and laughter
  Where the happy memories grow.